WHAT IT MEANS TO BE A
Teacher

A CELEBRATION OF THE
HUMOR, HEART, AND HERO
IN EVERY CLASSROOM

JENN LARSON

ADAMS MEDIA
NEW YORK   LONDON   TORONTO   SYDNEY   NEW DELHI

Adams Media
An Imprint of Simon & Schuster, Inc.
57 Littlefield Street
Avon, Massachusetts 02322

First Adams Media hardcover edition April 2020

ADAMS MEDIA and colophon are trademarks of Simon & Schuster.

For information about special discounts for bulk purchases, please contact Simon & Schuster Special Sales at 1-866-506-1949 or business@simonandschuster.com.

The Simon & Schuster Speakers Bureau can bring authors to your live event. For more information or to book an event contact the Simon & Schuster Speakers Bureau at 1-866-248-3049 or visit our website at www.simonspeakers.com.

Interior design by Colleen Cunningham, Erin Alexander, Julia Jacintho, and Harini Rajagopalan
Interior images © Getty Images; 123RF

Manufactured in China

10 9 8 7 6 5 4 3 2 1

Library of Congress Cataloging-in-Publication Data has been applied for.

ISBN 978-1-5072-1248-6
ISBN 978-1-5072-1249-3 (ebook)

For my brother, Dr. Brett Schmoll,
one of the most inspiring teachers I know.

Acknowledgments

I would like to thank Julia Jacques, Sarah Doughty, and the entire team at Simon & Schuster, Inc., who worked so hard to make this book a reality.

I am forever grateful for the tremendous love and support of my family, whose enthusiasm for this project never wavered.

Lastly, I am indebted to all of the amazing teachers I've been fortunate enough to have. You helped inspire a love of learning in me that continues to this day.

Introduction

Do you relish the sight of an empty "to be graded" pile?

Do you have a hiding spot for your "good markers"?

Do you strive to make a difference...Every. Single. Day?

If you do, you might be a teacher!

Teaching truly is an amazing career, although some would say that it's more of a calling. After all, how many other professions have the ability to impact lives and create a real change in the world? You probably live for those times when a struggling student finally "gets it," a reluctant reader falls in love with a book, or the entire class comes together to make the new kid feel welcome. Those are the moments that make it worthwhile. But teaching isn't all apples and color-coordinated school supplies, and in more challenging times, just knowing you're not alone helps. That's where *What It Means to Be a Teacher* comes in!

Here you'll find more than 150 entries designed to lift you up when you've had a bad day, make you laugh out loud (or shake your head in solidarity), and inspire you to keep going no matter what—because what you do matters more than you'll ever know.

So if you have enough coffee mugs to use a different one each day of the month, raise one up! If you are just *slightly* obsessed with Flair pens, sticky notes, or colored bins, stand up and be seen. If you ever use your teacher voice when you're *not* in the classroom, know that you're not the only one! And if you're ready to celebrate everything that it takes to be a teacher, dive in to this book and enjoy!

Favorite teachers are remembered FOREVER.

RAISE YOUR HAND
IF YOU'VE EVER FELT

PERSONALLY

VICTIMIZED

BY A STUDENT'S
DRAWING OF YOU.

TEACHER:

OPTIMIST
MENTOR
AWAKENER
FACILITATOR
CHAMPION
ENLIGHTENER
ENCOURAGER.

A teacher's favorite moments in the classroom aren't about the most fabulous lessons or the most beautiful bulletin boards.

Favorite moments happen when a shy student speaks up, a difficult student shows kindness, or a new student finds a friend.

AN EMPTY
"TO BE GRADED"
PILE LASTS ABOUT
AS LONG AS
AN EMPTY
LAUNDRY BASKET.

Teachers
who turn the
ordinary into
FUN
are my kind
of teachers.

Teachers may share knowledge every day, but don't ask them to share

THEIR GOOD MARKERS

YOU WERE

BORN

TO BE A TEACHER.
YOU ARE

WHERE

YOU SHOULD BE,
DOING WHAT YOU WERE

MEANT

TO DO.

THE *FASTEST* LAND ANIMAL?

A *TEACHER* AT RECESS, HEADING TO THE RESTROOM.

WHEN YOU BUILD STRONG RELATIONSHIPS WITH YOUR STUDENTS, AND THEY LOVE COMING TO SCHOOL,

THAT'S MAGIC.

You might be a teacher if...

You know the *magical curing powers* of a wet paper towel.

SOME OF THE
BEST TEACHERS
GOT THEIR START
WHEN THEY WERE
CHILDREN

TEACHING
STUFFED ANIMALS
AND DOLLS.

TEACHERS: HELPING THE ECONOMY, ONE DOLLAR-STORE TRIP AT A TIME.

REMEMBER, WITHOUT THE TEACHERS WHO INFLUENCED YOU, YOU WOULDN'T BE THE PERSON—OR TEACHER— YOU ARE TODAY.

SOMETIMES IN **TEACHING,** IT'S THE LITTLE THINGS THAT COUNT... LIKE **APRIL FOOLS' DAY** FALLING ON THE WEEKEND.

Teachers
may or may not
see the harvest,
but they are
seed planters
nonetheless.

STRANGE THINGS TEACHERS FIND THEMSELVES SAYING:

"Don't sharpen your finger."

"I'm sure giraffes get constipated just like humans do."

"Who's barking?"

"You need to hold your balls the entire way down the hallway and out to recess, or they will be mine."

"Is that a **frog** in your pocket?"

One of the **BEST SOUNDS** in a classroom is that of **STUDENTS WORKING TOGETHER.**

MY ODDS OF WINNING

POWERBALL

AND MY ODDS OF HAVING
ALL OF MY STUDENTS
LISTEN TO DIRECTIONS
THE FIRST TIME
ARE THE SAME.

Every day in classrooms big and small, *teachers are making a difference* in the lives of their students. It may be quiet and often go unnoticed, but it is a difference just the same *and it matters.*

Which would you choose?

A

Pencils would always be plentiful and would never need to be sharpened.

B

You would never have recess duty, bus duty, or indoor recess.

C

All staff meetings would be done via email.

D

All papers would grade themselves.

THE HE♥RT OF A

TEACHER

WEARS A CAPE.

Glittertastrophe

noun /gli dər tas trə fē/

A common winter holiday occurrence when a teacher uses glitter optimistically, but the glitter goes everywhere and is found on everything for weeks to come.

"I had my students create snow globes, but the custodian wasn't pleased with the *glittertastrophe* they created."

MAY YOU HAVE

THE CREATIVITY OF
MS. FRIZZLE,

THE PATIENCE OF MISS BINNEY,

THE *kindness* OF *Miss Honey,*

THE WISDOM OF
PROFESSOR DUMBLEDORE.

HINT:

A LOT OF TEACHERS

ALSO LOVE
CHOCOLATE.

»»»They can't live on apples alone!«««

A FORMER STUDENT'S SWEET NOTE, VISIT, OR HUG IS ONE OF THE GREATEST TEACHER JOYS!

I'M WORKING ON MY
LESSON PLANS...
RIGHT AFTER I CHECK
MY

email,

Facebook,

Pinterest, AND

Instagram

REAL
QUICK.

Every teacher
is different.
Find your own
teaching style.

Be your
best you!

Dear Tired Teacher,

Your days are focused on the needs of your students and your family♥ Don't forget to also take some time to focus on yourself♥ When you recharge, you not only feel better, but are also better able to help others too♥

Being
allowed to control
the thermostat
in your classroom
should be part
of the job
description.

DAY IN AND DAY OUT,
TEACHERS CARE.

THEY *plan* LESSONS,
connect WITH STUDENTS,
AND *teach* LIKE NOBODY'S BUSINESS.

THEY PUT THEIR HEARTS INTO
THEIR CLASSROOMS BECAUSE
THEY CARE... *every day.*

RATIONAL BRAIN

"I HAVE PLENTY OF BASKETS AND BOXES."

TEACHER BRAIN

"If I only had more baskets and boxes, I could really organize this classroom."

TEACHERS

ARE SOME OF THE MOST

COURAGEOUS

PEOPLE OUT THERE.

YOU MIGHT BE A TEACHER IF...

YOU SOMETIMES GET THE URGE TO REDIRECT

MISBEHAVING

KIDS IN PUBLIC PLACES.

Having high expectations and truly believing that students can succeed are the marks of an excellent teacher.

"Line up if you're wearing blue."

WHAT THEY HEARD

"Tell your neighbor that blue
is your favorite color.
Ask the teacher if it counts if
you're wearing blue underwear,
your mom was wearing
blue this morning,
or you wore blue yesterday."

ALL IT TAKES TO SEND AN ENTIRE CLASS INTO A FULL-BLOWN SPIRAL IS THE DISCOVERY OF ONE WELL-PLACED SPIDER OR INSECT.

TEACHING MAY BE ONE OF THE MOST DIFFICULT BUT REWARDING PR♥FESSIONS.

I need to find
hobbies that don't
include Flair pens
or laminating.

COPIER TIPS:

1. APPROACH THE COPIER SLOWLY, WITHOUT A SENSE OF HURRY.

2. WHEN YOU HAVE THE URGE TO SCREAM, CURSE, OR SLAM DOORS, WHISPER GENTLY INSTEAD.

3. COPIERS RESPOND WELL TO POSITIVE REINFORCEMENT. AS YOU PICK UP YOUR COPIES TO LEAVE, THANK THE COPIER AND WALK AWAY SLOWLY.

The art of teaching CAN BE FOUND IN THE LESSONS THAT GO SIDEWAYS BUT ARE successfully rescued.

You have a soft spot in your heart for your most difficult student.

Teacher Fact

You say **coffee,**
I say
teacher
fuel.

THERE'S A FINE LINE BETWEEN HOARDER & TEACHER, BUT SOMETIMES I'M WILLING TO CROSS IT.

NEVER UNDERESTIMATE THE POWER OF THE TEACHER-EYE.

It's impossible to reach every
student every day, no matter
how hard we may try.

We can't give up though:

We have to realize
that every now and then,
the stars will align,

and we will impact a student
more than we'll ever know.

ME

"I'M SO TIRED. I CAN'T WAIT TO PUT ON MY PAJAMAS AND GO TO SLEEP."

ALSO ME

"I JUST CAN'T FALL ASLEEP. WHY CAN'T THEY UNDERSTAND LONG DIVISION...? MAYBE I SHOULD GET RID OF MY TEACHER'S DESK... I WONDER IF THE DOLLAR STORE HAS ANYTHING NEW I CAN USE IN THE CLASSROOM..."

TEACHERS

encourage, *guide*,
inspire, NURTURE,
CREATE, PREPARE,
model, instill, develop,
persist, question,
ILLUMINATE,
mentor, LOVE,
MOTIVATE,
AND enlighten.

Every
classroom
has a miniature
Bermuda Triangle
where EXPO markers,
erasers, glue caps,
and black crayons
magically disappear.

TEACHERS ARE HUMANS.

SOMETIMES THEY FAIL MISERABLY. BUT THEY GET UP EACH DAY AND GREET THEIR STUDENTS WITH A SMILE AND THEY KEEP ON TEACHING,

BECAUSE THAT'S WHAT THEY WERE CALLED TO DO.

Candypocalypse

noun /kan dē päk əˌlips/

The day after any major holiday involving candy, such as Halloween, when kids are either climbing the walls or lazing in a sugar-induced coma.

"It was hard to keep the students engaged due to the ***candypocalypse*** they created.**"**

WHEN A TEACHER ENJOYS TEACHING,

kids just know.

TECHNOLOGY IS AN
AMAZING
EDUCATIONAL TOOL...

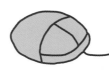

UNTIL YOU COUNT ON IT FOR AN ENTIRE ACTIVITY,
IT DECIDES NOT TO WORK, AND THIRTY SETS OF
EYES ARE WATCHING WHILE YOU TRY TO FIX IT.

Keep a box of the pictures students draw for you, their sweet notes, and their letters of appreciation.

When you're feeling discouraged, take out the contents of the box and look at them.

You might be a teacher if...

You know it's a full moon without even looking at the night sky.

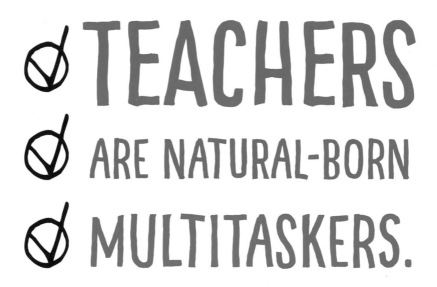

✓ TEACHERS ARE NATURAL-BORN MULTITASKERS.

IS THERE A YOUTUBE TUTORIAL ON HOW TO MAKE THE PERFECT SEATING CHART FOR A CLASSROOM WITH LIMITED SPACE, SWEET BUT CHATTY KIDS, AND A NUMBER OF POSSIBLE LAND MINE STUDENT COMBINATIONS, SO EVERYONE CAN SIT CLOSE TO THE FRONT?

Listen to your heart. You *know* what's best for *your* students.

1. DENIAL

2. ANGER

3. BARGAINING

4. DEPRESSION

5. ACCEPTANCE

The stages of getting ready to grade papers.

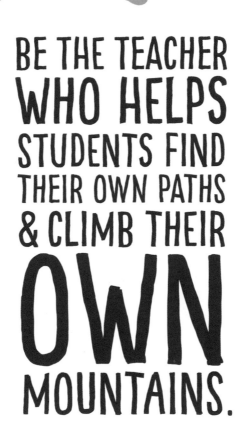

BE THE TEACHER WHO HELPS STUDENTS FIND THEIR OWN PATHS & CLIMB THEIR OWN MOUNTAINS.

Today's field trip is brought to you by the number

That's the number I counted 516 times to make sure no one was missing.

CREATING

MOTIVATED LEARNERS

IS ONE OF THE

GREATEST GIFTS

OF BEING A TEACHER.

YOU CAN'T BUY HAPPINESS...
BUT YOU CAN BUY SCHOOL SUPPLIES, AND THAT'S KIND OF THE SAME THING.

Sometimes TEACHING *isn't* PERFORMING MIRACLES; IT'S JUST PLAIN & PERSISTENCE HARD WORK!

The look on a student's face when they **SEE A TEACHER IN A PUBLIC PLACE** is similar to the expression of a scientist spotting **A RARE ANIMAL IN THE WILD.**

ONLY A

TEACHER

>>> TRULY <<<
UNDERSTANDS
WHAT IT TAKES
TO BE A
TEACHER.

Laryngitis

is a teaching game-changer.

The little things
we do as teachers—

a smile,

A KIND WORD,

a high-five–

are connections that mean
so much to our students.

SCHOLASTIC BONUS POINTS ARE THE

frequent-flier miles

OF TEACHING.

We only have our students **FOR** a short period of time.

WE HAVE NO IDEA WHAT THEIR FUTURES HOLD.

We can only focus **ON** equipping them in **THE** best way that we can while they're in our classrooms.

One ADVANTAGE of teaching: You can clock 10,000 STEPS BY LUNCH-TIME.

YOU CAN BE *WILD* ABOUT YOUR STUDENTS *& WILD* ABOUT YOUR WEEKENDS.

One of a teacher's greatest strengths is the ability to make split-second decisions...

All.

Day.

Long.

REGARDLESS OF YOUR **AMOUNT** OF **TEACHING EXPERIENCE,** EVERY YEAR *is a new year,* WITH **NEW STUDENTS,** WHO HAVE A *new set* OF **ABILITIES** AND **PERSONALITIES.**

STRANGE THINGS TEACHERS FIND THEMSELVES SAYING:

"Take the marshmallows out of your socks."

"Please stop choking him. He doesn't like it."

"Stop being a sheep and do your work please."

"I have to pee too, but we're taking a test now. Just think about the desert."

"Take the pickles off your eyes."

TEACHERS WHO

laugh easily & *laugh often*

ARE ABLE TO CREATE HAPPY CLASSROOMS.

TEACHING REQUIRES THE **KIND OF DETERMINATION** THAT CAN PERSEVERE THROUGH MULTIPLE **INTERCOM INTERRUPTIONS,** THE ONSET OF POURING RAIN, **AND A RANDOM** HONEYBEE'S FLIGHT **AROUND THE CLASSROOM.**

Take time to notice the little ways your students are

growing

each day.

Celebrate small victories.

ME

"I'M NOT NERVOUS ABOUT
MY UPCOMING OBSERVATION
AT ALL."

ALSO ME

*STAYS AWAKE UNTIL TWELVE A.M.
THINKING ABOUT IT.*

Teachers,

DON'T LET AN OFF DAY DEFINE YOU.

GET BACK UP,

BRUSH YOURSELF OFF,

AND KEEP GOING.

Your students feel like they know a secret when they find out your first name.

Teacher Fact

A

single teacher

WHO CARES

CAN HELP TURN A

CHILD'S LIFE

AROUND.

CONTESTANTS MUST

PLAN, TEACH, GRADE, & ADMINISTER TESTING

DURING THE SPRING FEVER SEASON.

AMAZING THINGS HAPPEN WHEN *teachers work in a* SCHOOL WITH A SUPPORTIVE *learning community.*

WHEN YOU'VE *finally* SAVED ENOUGH MONEY FOR A *vacation*— AND A STUDENT'S FAMILY IS ON THE SAME PLANE, HEADING TO THE SAME HOTEL...

A GOOD

TEACHER

CARES ABOUT THE

education

OF A CHILD.
A GREAT TEACHER

CARES ABOUT THE WHOLE CHILD.

Your students may call you "Mom" or "Dad" by mistake, and you may answer to it.

Teacher Fact

One of the hardest things about being a teacher is that **from** the time your students arrive, **until** they leave at the end of the day, **you are** on.

If you've never
washed pants with
POCKETS
FULL OF RANDOM
ITEMS
FROM SCHOOL,
are you even a teacher?

TEACHER

is just another word for

difference-maker.

You might be a
teacher if...

You can read
writing that is

UPSIDE DOWN.

NEVER UNDERESTIMATE THE POWER OF *teacher friendships.* HAVING A KINDRED SPIRIT WHO ≥UNDERSTANDS≤ YOU, ≥SUPPORTS≤ YOU, AND ≥WANTS THE BEST≤ FOR YOU MAKES A HUGE *difference.*

ME

"THE END OF THE YEAR IS EXHAUSTING! JUST A FEW MORE WEEKS 'TIL SUMMER."

ALSO ME

"I CAN'T WAIT TO SET UP MY CLASSROOM FOR BACK-TO-SCHOOL."

If you would like to be a student in **YOUR** class, you're doing something right!

ME

"I AM DOING SO WELL ON MY DIET.
I ALREADY LOST 8 POUNDS."

ALSO ME

"IS THERE ANY CAKE LEFT
IN THE TEACHERS' LOUNGE?"

Each
student
is in your
classroom
for a
reason.

Which would you choose?

A

None of the calories consumed in the teachers' lounge would count.

B

You could use the restroom as needed during the school day.

C

Report cards would fill themselves out.

D

All parents would read class newsletters.

Some days, you feel like a teaching rock star, **while other days,** you may doubt that you're reaching your students. **Remember** that what you're doing as a teacher means so much!

ONLY TEACHERS KNOW THAT THE $DOLLAR STORE CAN EASILY TURN INTO THE HUNDRED-DOLLAR STORE.

A **TEACHER** IS

 A NURSE

 A COUNSELOR

 A MANAGER

 A COACH

 A MEDIATOR

 AN INVESTIGATOR

 AN ACTOR

 A JUDGE

 A WRITER

 AN EVENTS COORDINATOR

 A CHEERLEADER

 A COMEDIAN

 A TECHNICIAN

 A LIBRARIAN

 A PUBLIC RELATIONS SPECIALIST

 AN ARTIST

AN EDUCATOR

IndoorRecessobia

noun /in dôr rē ses ō bē ə/

The constant fear that students will be kept in from recess for an extended period of time due to poor weather conditions.

" This week, when the forecast called for continuous rain, I started to develop *IndoorRecessobia*.**"**

TEACHERS

WHO WORRY ABOUT BEING THE KIND OF TEACHER KIDS NEED ARE THE

BEST KIND OF

TEACHERS.

You might be a teacher if...

You have perfected the staff meeting poker face.

A TEACHER IS AN *Optimist* WHO TRULY *Believes* THAT ALL STUDENTS CAN REACH THEIR *Potential.*

Buying School Supplies

STUFF YOU ACTUALLY NEED

STUFF YOU MIGHT NEED THAT'S ON SALE

STUFF YOU BUY BECAUSE IT'S CUTE AND IT MAKES YOU HAPPY

THE
BEST TEACHERS
constantly
LOOK FOR WAYS
TO MAKE THEIR LESSONS MORE
motivating
FOR THEIR STUDENTS.

STUDENT: *Raises hand.*

TEACHER: "Is this a question or a story?"

STUDENT: "It's a question...

So, yesterday I was riding my bike and then..."

#justanotherdayintheclassroom

You only have a
limited number of days
each school year.

Make every day count!

TEACHER-TIME IS RELATIVE.

5 MORE MINUTES COULD REALLY BE **2** MINUTES OR **15** MINUTES, DEPENDING UPON STUDENT FOCUS AND TEACHER MOOD.

Students gravitate
to teachers who radiate
a feeling of warmth, like
Sunshine.

When the classroom is a mess, a stack of math tests needs to be graded, lesson plans need to be done, and pencils need to be sharpened—but instead you sit at your desk, staring off into space.

A WISE TEACHER GIVES STUDENTS THE TOOLS TO BUILD THEIR OWN FOUNDATION FOR UNDERSTANDING.

You often have "schoolmares" the night before the first day of school each year.

Teacher Fact

One of the most exciting (but also challenging) parts of teaching is that it is not static: There is ALWAYS something NEW TO LEARN.

STRANGE THINGS TEACHERS FIND THEMSELVES SAYING:

"No, the eraser can't be pooped out if it disappears up your nose."

"Don't drink your watercolor water."

"The banana is not a weapon."

"Please stop screaming with your mouth closed. I can tell it's you."

"No, I don't know why dog farts are silent."

The CLASSROOM ISN'T NEARLY AS important AS THE Teacher.

The less time you spend preparing a lesson, the more likely it is an administrator will come into your classroom to observe it.

Teacher Fact

A **GOOD** TEACHER
TEACHES.

A **GREAT** TEACHER
INSPIRES.

NETFLIX

SHOULD HAVE A CATEGORY CALLED

"Easy to Follow While Grading Papers."

EACH NEW DAY
IN THE
CLASSROOM
IS AN
OPPORTUNITY
FOR A
FRESH START.

THE GREATEST
DETERRENT
FOR TAKING SICK LEAVE:
WRITING
LESSON PLANS
FOR A
SUBSTITUTE TEACHER.

EVERY TEACHER POSSESSES UNIQUE TALENTS & SKILLS that can be used to positively impact STUDENTS.

WHAT I SAID

66 If you finish your work early, you can read a book. 99

WHAT THEY HEARD

66 If you finish your work early, you can do anything you want: Chat with your neighbor, walk around the room aimlessly, make a tiny pencil, or twirl your ruler. 99

Smile at students—
the more often the better.

Smile when you first see them.

Smile when they're sharing
an accomplishment with you,
however small.

And definitely *smile* on the
first day of school.

Copyagious

noun /kä pē ā jəs/

When one student does something and it causes other students to do the same thing.

" After one student left to use the restroom, the whole class wanted to go, because of the **copyagious** effect. **"**

TEACHERS WHO BUILD Positive Relationships WITH STUDENTS CREATE A Strong Foundation FOR LEARNING.

OF COURSE WE
LOVE OUR STUDENTS,
BUT TEACHING DOES MAKE
YOU THINK LONG AND HARD
ABOUT WHICH NAMES YOU
CHOOSE FOR YOUR
OWN CHILDREN.

EACH DAY Teachers ARE DOING Amazing THINGS IN THE Classroom.

WHAT WE SAY TO OUR STUDENTS:

"I need everyone's attention right now.
Are you focusing?"

WHAT WE FOCUS ON AT STAFF MEETINGS:

So, if I put the chicken in the
oven when I get home, I can make
a salad while it's cooking...

Some days I amaze myself.

Other days, I wear two different shoes to school.

You might be a teacher if...

You know exactly who needs extra help and who needs enrichment, without looking at the data.

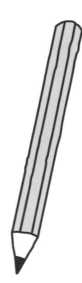

NEVER COMPARE
YOURSELF TO ANOTHER

TEACHER.

»»» YOU ARE «««

WORTHY

IN YOUR OWN RIGHT.
YOU ARE THE TEACHER
YOUR STUDENTS NEED.

CLASSROOM STATUS:

CURRENTLY EATING
THE LAST OF MY
SECRET CANDY STASH.

Teachers have the ABILITY to make a Student's Day, Simply with a KIND WORD or a bit of Encouragement.

ABOUT

90%

OF GRADING IS
SHAKING YOUR HEAD
AND ASKING,

"What were they thinking?"

TEACHERS

ROOT FOR THE

UNDERDOGS.

Do I need more prep time?

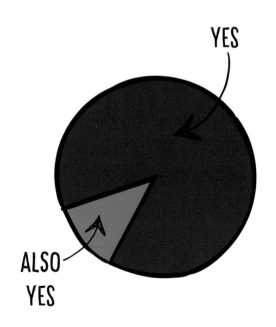

YES

ALSO
YES

Knowing
a teacher cares
is one of the
greatest gifts
we can give to our

students.

THAT MOMENT WHEN YOU REALIZE YOUR DRAWING ON THE BOARD COULD BE **MISINTERPRETED AS AN INAPPROPRIATE IMAGE.**

Teaching students TO **love learning** AND TO BE

CURI⌕US

about the world helps prepare them for the future.

Fact:

THE AVERAGE TEACHER HAS TO WAIT
ALL DAY
TO USE THE RESTROOM;

THE WOOD FROG
CAN HOLD ITS PEE FOR UP TO
EIGHT MONTHS.
LET THAT SINK IN.

Teaching is not for everyone. It takes a person who can deal with a certain level of

CHAOS,

tucked between moments of

brilliance,

to thrive.

TEACHING CERTIFICATES SHOULD COME WITH A

laminator,

personal copier,

Cricut machine,

& coffee maker.

TEACHERS PROVIDE **THE KNOWLEDGE, CRITICAL THINKING SKILLS, & HUMAN EXPERIENCES** THAT SHAPE **FUTURE LEADERS, INNOVATORS, CREATORS, AND MOTIVATORS.**

NO PRESSURE, THOUGH...

Once you truly master a set of curricula, it will be replaced.

GOOD TEACHERS KNOW THAT emotional learning AND academics go hand in hand.

Malcopyia

noun /mal kä pē ə/

When you jam the copy machine and are unable to fix the jam—so you have to leave it for the next unsuspecting teacher.

" I planned to make the class a set of worksheets this afternoon, but I had *malcopyia*.**"**

Be the teacher who welcomes all students with an open mind and open heart.

Just a seating chart?
Nope, it's rocket science.

$x^2+y^2=4$ $x^2+y^2=4$

$d=\sqrt{(8,5+2,3)^2+(0,7-4)^2}=$

$\sqrt{10,8^2+3,3^2}\approx 11,3$

$\frac{1}{2}(b+c),\ g=\frac{1}{3}(a+b+c)$

$|AB|:|BC|=\lambda:(1-\lambda)$

$\vec{AC}=(c\cdot o),\ \vec{AB}=\underline{b}-\underline{a}=\lambda(c\cdot o$

$b=(1-\lambda)g+\lambda c\quad \lambda=\frac{1}{2}$

$\underline{b}=\frac{1}{2}(\underline{a}+\underline{c})$

$|\underline{u}\wedge\underline{v}|=|\underline{u}||\underline{v}|\sin\theta$

$(\underline{u}\cdot\underline{v})^2+|\underline{u}\wedge\underline{v}|^2=|\underline{u}|^2|\underline{v}|^2$

$|\underline{u}\wedge\underline{v}|^2=|\underline{u}|^2|\underline{v}|^2\sin^2\theta$

$\underline{u}\wedge\underline{v}=|\underline{u}||\underline{v}|\sin\theta\underline{n}$

$y=b$
$b>0$
$b<0,\ y=0$
$x=f$

$y=3$ $x=-\frac{5}{3}$

$=0\quad b=3$

$b=-\frac{c}{B}$

$2,B=-4,C=5)$

$=-\frac{2}{-4}=0,5,\ b=\frac{-5}{-4}=1,25$

$(\theta,\varphi)\in[0,2\pi]\times$
$[-\pi/2,\pi/2]$

$m_1=2,\ m_2=3, x_1=6, y_1=-4, x_2=0, y_2=0,$

$x=\frac{18}{5}=3.6\quad y=-\frac{12}{5}=-2,4$

$\lambda=m_1:m_2=-2$

$m_1=-2,\ m_2=1\qquad m_1=2,\ m_2=-1$

$x=\frac{1\times 1+(-2)\times 3}{155}=5$

area A

$|\underline{u}||\underline{v}|\sin\theta$

$A_1(x_1;y_1)\quad A_2(x_2;y_2)$

$60°$

area A
$|\underline{u}||\underline{v}|\sin\theta$

CHANGES in educational policies MUST START WITH TEACHERS. THEY KNOW WHAT WORKS WELL— & what doesn't.

I MAY BE A COLLEGE-EDUCATED TEACHER, BUT WHEN I SPELL CERTAIN WORDS, I STILL THINK "WED-NES-DAY," "FEB-RU-ARY," "CAL-EN-DAR."

THE VERY BEST TEACHERS

FOCUS ON *growing* LEARNERS

WHILE *nurturing* HEARTS.

Which would you choose?

 A

Lesson plans would never be checked by an administrator and would only be written for yourself.

 B

The copy machine would never need toner and would work perfectly all the time.

 C

Every paper would be turned in with a name on it.

 D

You would get a planning day to yourself each week, so you would never have to bring work home.

WHEN YOU ARE *in love with teaching,* YOUR ENTHUSIASM PERMEATES EVERYTHING THAT GOES ON IN YOUR CLASSROOM.

ME

"I ONLY HAVE $16
IN MY BANK ACCOUNT."

ALSO ME

"I COULD SPEND IT ALL ON
SCHOOL SUPPLIES."

Teaching is about choices.

a **b** **c**

| What you will teach today and | how you will teach it... | what you will and won't allow... |

Hundreds of choices every day that impact students' experiences in your classroom.

TEACHING

AT THE END OF THE YEAR SHOULD COUNT AS AN

EXTREME

SPORT.

Some of the most dynamic teachers are entertainers at heart.

You might be a teacher if...

You are obsessed with comfortable shoes.

I'm thankful

TO BE THE ONE

THEY CALL

"teacher."

IF ONLY YOUR
TEACHER BAG
EARNED
FREQUENT-FLIER
MILES...

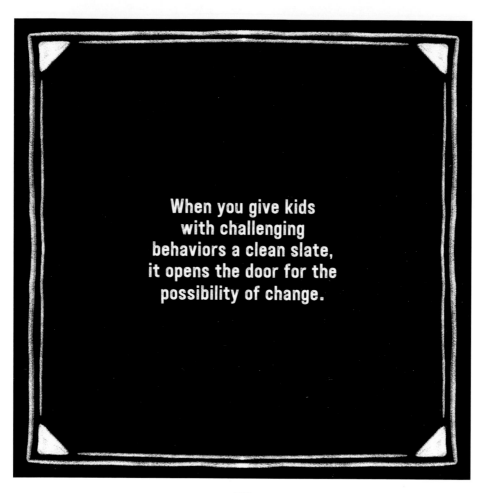

When you give kids
with challenging
behaviors a clean slate,
it opens the door for the
possibility of change.

Things I think about while monitoring testing:

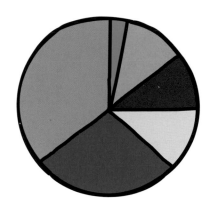

- ⬛ HOW MANY STEPS AM I GETTING?
- ⬛ WHO NEEDS A TISSUE?
- ⬛ I BETTER NOT HEAR TALKING
- ⬛ SERIOUSLY, YOU CAN'T BE FINISHED THIS QUICKLY
- ⬛ FOOD
- ⬛ WHEN WILL THIS BE OVER?

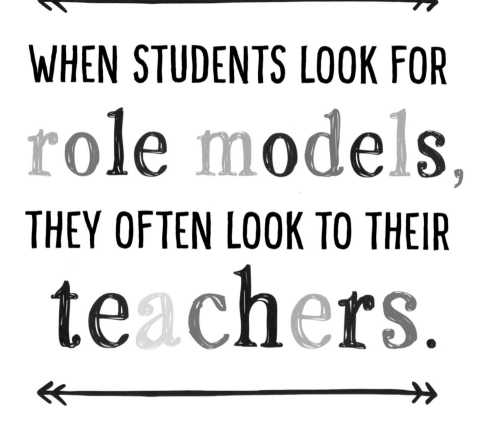

WHEN STUDENTS LOOK FOR role models, THEY OFTEN LOOK TO THEIR teachers.

You can still be a great teacher and have to be reminded to take attendance each day.

Every day, teachers educate multiple students with different abilities and different needs, while hitting educational standards, and trying to teach students to be better human beings.

What they do is miraculous.

STRANGE THINGS TEACHERS FIND THEMSELVES SAYING:

"Yes, even fish poop and pee."

"We don't lick the bottom of our shoes."

"Why am I hearing voices?"

"School is not the place to worry about your oily T-zone."

"Put the skunk down."

WHAT OTHER PROFESSION IS FOCUSED ON

SHAPING *THE* FUTURE

LIKE TEACHING IS?

BEING AN EDUCATOR IS BOTH A

PRIVILEGE *AND* A HUGE RESPONSIBILITY.

Your new hairstyle will **be** immediately noticed and judged by your students.

May you always have the

ENTHUSIASM AND ENERGY

of a first-year teacher, and the

ENDURANCE AND WISDOM

of a twenty-year teacher.

Breaknesia

noun   /brāk nē ZHə/

The complete and utter inability of students to remember a concept taught before a school break.

"The student wanted to answer the question about fractions, but he had *breaknesia*.**"**

PARENTS AND TEACHERS WHO WORK TOGETHER ARE **UN**STOPPABLE.

It's all fun and games until **IT'S SUNDAY NIGHT** and you realize that **YOUR TEACHER BAG** is still sitting untouched **BY THE DOOR.**

Teachers

WIDEN HORIZONS
& help students believe that
THEIR DREAMS
ARE POSSIBLE.

PARENT-TEACHER CONFERENCES ARE LITMUS TESTS FOR TEACHERS.

Teaching is not for the faint of heart.

It is complex, messy, challenging, and sometimes even disappointing.

But teaching is also an adventure that can bring great satisfaction in moments both big and small—with comfort in the knowledge that a teacher's life truly *makes a difference*.

ONLY A TEACHER
COULD GET
≥*excited*≤
BY A NEW PACK OF

EXPO MARKERS.

EXCELLENT TEACHERS

AREN'T PERFECT TEACHERS.

THEY ARE SIMPLY FOCUSED ON DOING WHAT THEY THINK IS BEST FOR THEIR STUDENTS, REGARDLESS OF THE OBSTACLES THEY MAY FACE.

STRANGE THINGS TEACHERS FIND THEMSELVES SAYING:

"Don't put your finger in your face holes."

"Please don't bring a pineapple into the computer lab."

"No, I don't want to smell your finger."

"How would you like it if someone smooshed down your Mohawk?"

"Stop singing into your corn dog."

Teachers WHO HOLD NOTHING BACK AND WHO TEACH *Whole-Heartedly* ARE THE *Passionate* Teachers STUDENTS NEED.

RECESS

IS A CONSTANT STRUGGLE BETWEEN

 the need to use the restroom,

 the need to grab a coffee,

 and the need to get something done.

TEACHERS *live in the* **PRESENT MOMENT** *of the* **CLASSROOM,** *in the hopes that what* **THEY DO** *extends well into* **THE FUTURE.**

LIFE'S BIGGEST MYSTERIES:

STONEHENGE

THE PYRAMIDS OF EGYPT

THE MOAI OF
EASTER ISLAND

THE PLACE WHERE ALL
THE PENCILS WENT

You might be a teacher if...

You feel like a combination of

CAMP COUNSELOR,

CRUISE DIRECTOR,

AND ZOOKEEPER

during the last week of school.

BE THE TEACHER
WHO MAKES KIDS
EXCITED
TO COME TO SCHOOL
EVERY DAY.

About the Author

Jenn Larson's parents were both teachers, so teaching is in her blood! She has a master's degree in curriculum and instruction and more than twenty years of experience as a teacher in the elementary classroom. Jenn is also a teacher-author, and she loves to share teaching tips for busy teachers—as well as resources for upper elementary students—on her website, *The Teacher Next Door*.